D0772785

Valentine's Day

by Rebecca Pettiford

Bullfrog Books

Ideas for Parents and Teachers

Bullfrog Books let children practice reading informational text at the earliest reading levels. Repetition, familiar words, and photo labels support early readers.

Before Reading

- Discuss the cover photo. What does it tell them?

- Look at the picture glossary together. Read and discuss the words.

Read the Book

- "Walk" through the book and look at the photos. Let the child ask questions. Point out the photo labels.

- Read the book to the child, or have him or her read independently.

After Reading

- Prompt the child to think more. Ask: How do you celebrate Valentine's Day? What sorts of things do you see when it's Valentine's Day?

Bullfrog Books are published by Jump!
5357 Penn Avenue South
Minneapolis, MN 55419
www.jumplibrary.com

Library of Congress Cataloging-in-Publication Data

Pettiford, Rebecca.
  Valentine's day / by Rebecca Pettiford.
    pages cm.—(Holidays)
  ISBN 978-1-62031-187-5 (hardcover: alk. paper)
  ISBN 978-1-62496-274-5 (ebook)
  1. Valentine's Day—Juvenile literature. I. Title.
  GT4925.P48 2016
  394.2618—dc23
                                            2014041413

Editor: Jenny Fretland VanVoorst
Series Designer: Ellen Huber
Book Designer: Lindaanne Donohoe
Photo Researcher: Jenny Fretland VanVoorst

Photo Credits: All photos by Shutterstock except: iStock, 8–9; SuperStock, 5, 6–7, 10, 15, 18–19, 20–21, 23br; Thinkstock, 3, 4, 16–17, 24.

Printed in the United States of America at Corporate Graphics in North Mankato, Minnesota.

Table of Contents

What Is Valentine's Day?

Valentine's Day
is February 14.

Many people celebrate it.

What do we do?

We give cards.

We give gifts.

We show love
for each other.

Henry makes a card.
It looks like a heart.
He gives it to Fay.

This card has Cupid on it.
Cupid is a symbol of love.

He has a bow and arrow.

Watch out!

If he shoots you,
you will fall in love!

Dad gives Mom roses.

She loves them!

They kiss.

What does Eve have?
A box of candy.

She opens it.
It's chocolate!

15

Will loves Nina.

He gives her a gift.

What does Grace have?
A valentine.
It's for her mom.

Happy Valentine's Day!

Symbols of Valentine's Day

chocolates

roses

hearts

Cupid

Picture Glossary

arrow
A sharp stick that is shot from a bow.

symbol
A design, figure, or object that represents something else.

bow
A curved piece of wood from which an arrow is shot.

valentine
A card or gift that people give to a loved one on Valentine's Day.

Index

To Learn More

Learning more is as easy as 1, 2, 3.

1) Go to www.factsurfer.com

2) Enter "Valentinesday" into the search box.

3) Click the "Surf" button to see a list of websites.

With factsurfer.com, finding more information is just a click away.

24